LET'S FIND OUT! *LIFE SCIENCE*

WHAT IS A LIFE CYCLE?

LOUISE SPILSBURY

Britannica®
Educational Publishing

IN ASSOCIATION WITH

ROSEN
EDUCATIONAL SERVICES

Published in 2014 by Britannica Educational Publishing (a trademark of Encyclopædia Britannica, Inc.) in association with The Rosen Publishing Group, Inc.
29 East 21st Street, New York, NY 10010

Distributed exclusively by Rosen Publishing.
To see additional Britannica Educational Publishing titles, go to rosenpublishing.com

First Edition

Britannica Educational Publishing
J.E. Luebering: Director, Core Reference Group
Anthony L. Green: Editor, Compton's by Britannica

Rosen Publishing
Hope Lourie Killcoyne: Executive Editor
Nelson Sá: Art Director

Library of Congress Cataloging-in-Publication Data

Spilsbury, Louise
What is a life cycle? / Louise Spilsbury. — First edition.
    pages cm. — (Let's find out. Life science)
Audience: Grades 3 to 6.
Includes bibliographical references and index.
ISBN 978-1-62275-231-7 (library binding) — ISBN 978-1-62275-234-8 (pbk.) — ISBN 978-1-62275-235-5 (6-pack)
1. Life cycles (Biology)—Juvenile literature. I. Title.
QH501.S655 2014
571.8—dc23

                                                                2013026794

Manufactured in the United States of America.

Photo credits
Cover: Istockphoto: Stanley45 bg; Shutterstock: Marco Uliana fg. Inside: Dreamstime: AGLphotoproductions 20, Crookid 12–13, Ecophoto 21, Jpsdk 10, Kikkerdirk 11, Kjuuurs 22, Kts 7, Mb2006 13, Onefivenine 9, Photogaga 28, Rbbrdckybk 15, Robgubiani 23, Sarahtheo 24, Sdenness 8, Showface 6, Tjkphotography 17, Wizzard 25, Xenomanes 27; Istockphoto: Stanley45 1bg; Shutterstock: Andresr 5, BMJ 18–19, Jo Crebbin 19, EcoPrint 4, Heiko Kiera 16, Levent Konuk 14, Alan Lucas 29, StevenRussellSmithPhotos 26, Marco Uliana 1fg.

CONTENTS

STAGES IN LIFE

A life cycle is the stages in the life of a living thing. Living things are born, grow into adults that can have their own babies, and eventually die. The babies grow into adults and have more young, and so the life cycles continue.

⏩ **Male giraffes fight to win the right to have babies with a female giraffe.**

Many living things are small and weak when they are first born. They face dangers, such as animals that want to eat them. As living things grow into adults, they become bigger and stronger. Then they are able to have and care for their own young.

▶▶

Human babies develop inside their mother's body for nine months. Most parents care for their children for up to 18 years after birth, if not longer.

THINK ABOUT IT
Reproduction is when animals have babies. It is an essential part of life cycles. What would be the effect if living things could not reproduce and have young?

Flowers

A plant's flowers are an important part of its life cycle. Inside a flower there are male and female parts. The male parts make a powder called pollen. When pollen from one flower moves to the female part of another flower, a seed starts to grow in the flower. One day, this seed might grow into a new plant.

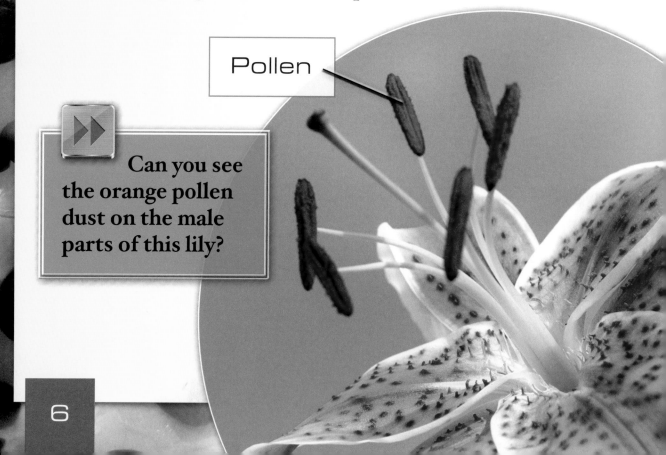

Pollen

Can you see the orange pollen dust on the male parts of this lily?

Some plants use animals to move their pollen. Flowers contain a sugary juice called nectar. When birds and bees feed on the nectar, pollen rubs onto the animals. The pollen rubs off again when the animals visit another flower. Some plants use the wind to pollinate their flowers.

Pollinate means to move pollen from the male parts of one flower to the female parts of another.

When a hummingbird feeds on nectar, it helps to move the flower's pollen from one plant to another.

SEED TO PLANT

After seeds start to develop in a plant, the flowers die. Fruits grow around the seeds. Fruits protect the seeds and help them to spread. Animals eat soft fruits such as berries. The seeds come out in their droppings.

Some fruits are hard. They have hooks in them to catch onto an animal's fur when it brushes past.

Dandelion seeds have feathery fruits shaped like parachutes to help them fly to a new place.

THINK ABOUT IT
Why do you think some seeds move to a new place, away from their parent plant, to grow?

A new plant starts to grow from a seed.

When a seed lands on the ground, it waits until the conditions are right for it to begin to grow. When it is warm and wet, the seed splits open and the plant starts to sping up. It develops leaves and gets bigger. When it is fully grown, the plant grows flowers and makes its own seeds.

INSECTS

Some baby insects hatch from eggs, but they look nothing like their parents until they reach the adult stage of life. Beetles, bees, ants, moths, and butterflies go through four life stages: egg, larva, pupa, and adult. They look different in each stage. This process of change is called **metamorphosis**.

A larva, called a caterpillar, hatches from a butterfly egg. Then it makes a shell to live in during the pupa stage, while it changes into an adult butterfly.

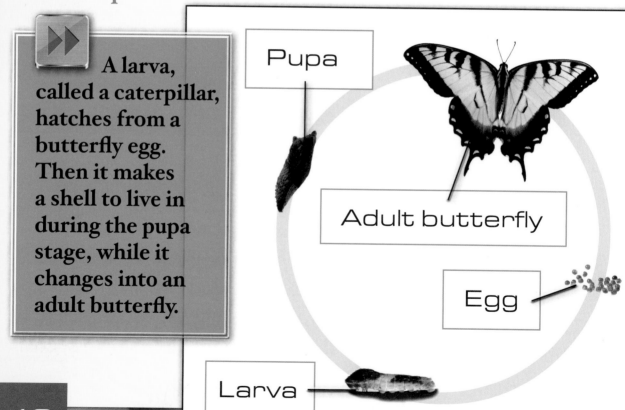

Pupa

Adult butterfly

Egg

Larva

Insects such as grasshoppers and cockroaches go through three life stages. They begin life as eggs. Then they hatch from the eggs, usually as smaller versions of the adults. The insects then grow into adults.

Some insects change by growing wings. Young dragonflies hatch and live in the water until they grow wings and become adults.

Metamorphosis means the way animals change appearance during their life cycles.

Adult dragonflies are brightly colored, but young dragonflies have duller colors to blend in with rocks and sand.

Amphibians

Frogs, toads, and other amphibians start their life cycles in water. When they are adults, some move onto land though most stay in water. Because amphibians live in water and on land, their natural environments are shores, ponds, marshes, swamps, and low-lying meadows.

Frogs lay thousands of eggs, usually in the water. After a few weeks, tadpoles hatch out of the eggs. The tadpoles have no legs and they have a tail. They feed on small underwater plants.

Tadpoles can breathe underwater, like fish.

COMPARE AND CONTRAST
Think about tadpoles and adult frogs. Why do you think adult frogs have webbed feet?

An adult frog can live on land or in water.

Tadpoles change as they grow. First, they grow back legs and lungs and come to the water's surface to breathe air. Then, they grow front legs and lose their tail, becoming frogs. The cycle begins again when the frogs lay their eggs.

Fish

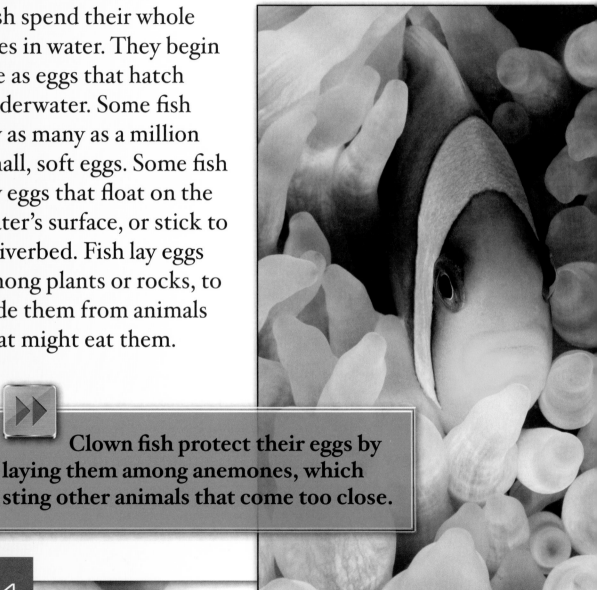

Fish spend their whole lives in water. They begin life as eggs that hatch underwater. Some fish lay as many as a million small, soft eggs. Some fish lay eggs that float on the water's surface, or stick to a riverbed. Fish lay eggs among plants or rocks, to hide them from animals that might eat them.

Clown fish protect their eggs by laying them among anemones, which sting other animals that come too close.

Female sea horses lay their eggs in a pouch on the male sea horse's body. The male keeps the eggs safe until they are ready to hatch.

Most fish swim away after laying their eggs. The young fish that hatch out of the eggs grow up alone. At first they are very small and cannot swim fast, so many are eaten by other animals. Fish are less likely to be eaten when they become adults.

THINK ABOUT IT
Why do you think adult fish lay so many eggs at a time?

Reptiles

Alligators, snakes, and turtles are reptiles. To reproduce, most reptiles lay eggs. The eggs contain a yolk for food, but **embryos** also need to be kept warm and safe. Sea turtles crawl onto beaches and bury their eggs under sand. Alligators lay their eggs under a pile of plants. The plants make heat as they rot.

Reptiles, such as snakes, lay soft, leathery eggs on land.

Embryos are living things in their first stages of growth.

Young reptiles that hatch out of eggs look like small versions of adult reptiles, but many never see their parents. Most reptiles leave the eggs after laying them, so the babies must care for themselves.

Alligators and crocodiles carry their newly-hatched young to the water, where the adults mostly live. They care for the young until they are old enough to live alone.

Crocodiles carry their babies very gently between their teeth!

Birds

Birds build nests from objects such as grass, twigs, and mud. Then they lay eggs, which have hard shells, in the nests. Birds sit on the eggs to keep them warm while the embryos inside grow and get ready to hatch.

Some birds do not make nests. Emperor penguins live in Antarctica where there are no materials to make nests.

COMPARE AND CONTRAST
Think about reptile and bird eggs, and how the adults care for their eggs.

Emperor penguins keep their eggs warm by resting them on their feet and tucking them beneath their stomachs.

Most chicks that hatch out of bird eggs are small, have no feathers, and are helpless. Their parents keep them warm, bring them food, and protect them from other animals, such as eagles. Gradually the chicks grow feathers and get bigger and stronger until they are ready to leave the nest and fly away.

Herons catch fish and fly back to their nests to feed their chicks.

Mammals

Mammals such as cats, apes, and humans develop inside the mother's body. By doing so, they can develop more fully before they are born. Fully developed babies are safer at birth than less-developed babies. For example, baby giraffes are ready to run just a few hours after being born. This means they can run away from danger.

Newborn mice cannot walk, feed, or care for themselves.

Mammal parents care for their young. A female mammal feeds her baby with milk from her body. This helps it to grow until it can feed itself. One or both parents protect the baby from danger. Many young mammals stay with their parents for a long time, to learn the skills they need to survive.

THINK ABOUT IT
Animals that care for young for a long time have fewer babies than animals that care for young for a short time. Why do you think this is?

▶▶ Female baboons carry their babies everywhere!

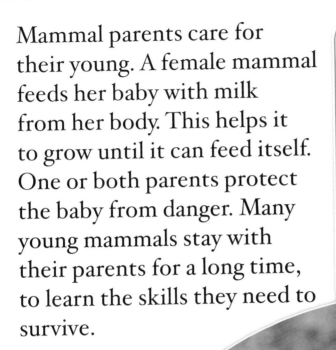

21

UNUSUAL MAMMALS

Some mammals have unusual life cycles. Female kangaroos and other marsupials have short pregnancies of about six weeks. The embryo is born early and then continues to develop in a pouch on its mother's stomach. It feeds on milk, sleeps, and grows. Often, after a baby kangaroo is ready to leave the pouch, it hops back in again, to feel safe and warm.

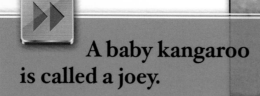

A baby kangaroo is called a joey.

A spiny anteater hatches from an egg inside its mother's pouch.

Two very unusual mammals lay eggs. Female spiny anteaters lay a single egg in a pouch. When the baby hatches, it feeds and grows to 500 times its original size. Then it leaves the pouch. A female duck-billed platypus lays an egg in a burrow. When the baby hatches, it feeds on its mother's milk.

A **burrow** is a tunnel or hole that an animal digs to have young in, or to live in.

DIFFERENT PLACES

The life cycles of some living things happen in different places. Salmon travel very far during their life cycle. Babies hatch from eggs in rivers and streams. Then they swim thousands of miles to the ocean. They grow and live in the ocean for up to seven years. As adults, they swim back to rivers and streams to reproduce.

A salmon's life cycle is complete once it has reproduced. Then the salmon dies.

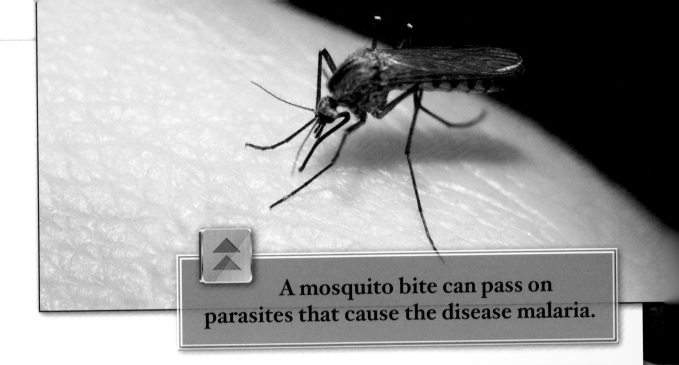

A mosquito bite can pass on parasites that cause the disease malaria.

Some animals complete part of their life cycle inside other living things. Malaria **parasites** are so small we cannot see them. When infected mosquitoes bite an animal to feed on its blood, malaria parasites swim from the mosquito's stomach into the victim's blood. There, parasites feed, grow, and reproduce inside the blood of the animal that was bitten.

Parasites are living things that live on or in another living thing, and often harm it.

DEATH

Death is the end of a life cycle. Some living things are born, grow, have young, and die rapidly. Some plants grow from seeds, grow flowers, and die in one season. A young mayfly hatches from an egg on the riverbed, living for up to two years underwater. It leaves the water as an adult. Once it was thought that they lived only a single day, but more careful study has shown that they may remain alive somewhat longer.

THINK ABOUT IT
Humans live longer than most other mammals. Today, people live longer than they did in the past. Why do you think this might be?

▶▶ An adult mayfly has a short life.

Some living things have life cycles that last for many years. Elephants can live for 70 years, and some humans have lived to be more than 100 years old. The llareta plant, which is found in the Atacama Desert in Chile, can live for thousands of years.

>> **Parts of this llareta plant are more than 3,000 years old.**

Dangers

Living things face dangers that can stop them from completing their life cycles. Some animals face danger from other animals. Lions hunt zebra, foxes eat rabbits, and bats eat flies. Plants die early in dry places, where they cannot get the water they need to make food. Birds may die if a storm washes away their nest.

Hungry bears catch salmon as the fish swim up rivers to reproduce.

By feeding this baby elephant, people are helping it to survive.

COMPARE AND CONTRAST
Think about some of the life cycles in this book. What are their similarities and differences?

Humans can cause harm to other living things. When people cut down trees to clear land for farms, animals lose their homes and food. When people kill mother elephants for their tusks, their babies die. Other people help animals. They plant trees, try to stop hunting, or care for baby animals. These people help living things to complete their life cycles!

GLOSSARY

amphibians Animals that hatch from an egg underwater and live on land or water as an adult. Frogs and toads are examples of amphibians.

anemones Meat-eating animals that live in the ocean. Anemones look like plants.

conditions The environment surrounding something.

eggs Protective containers in which baby animals start to grow.

female A living thing that can produce eggs, seeds, or babies.

fruits The parts of a plant that holds its seeds.

insects Small animals such as flies, ants, or beetles.

larva The stage of growth of some insects after hatching from an egg.

male A living thing that reproduces with a female.

mammals Animals that give birth to live babies and feed their young on milk from their bodies. Humans, dogs, and apes are examples of mammals.

marsupials Mammals that have a tiny baby that develops in a pouch on the mother's body. Kangaroos are marsupials.

nectar A sugary juice found in the middle of a flower.

pollen A powder that is found inside a flower.

pupa The stage of growth that occurs between when an insect is a larva and an adult.

reproduction To have young or babies.

reptiles Animals with hard, scaly skin. Reptiles lay soft eggs. Snakes and chameleons are examples of reptiles.

seed The part of a plant that produces another plant.

webbed feet Feet with skin stretched between them.

yolk Food found inside an egg. The yolk nourishes an embryo.

FOR MORE INFORMATION

Books

Aloian, Molly. *Life Cycles of Insects* (Insects Close-Up). New York, NY: Crabtree Publishing Company, 2013.

Callery, Sean. *Life Cycles: River.* London, UK: Kingfisher, 2013.

Head, Honor. *Plants* (Amazing Life Cycles). London, UK: Ticktock Books, 2013.

Prior, Jennifer. *The Human Life Cycle* (TIME for Kids Nonfiction Readers). Huntington Beach, CA: Teacher Created Materials, 2011.

Reilly, Kathleen M. *Explore Life Cycles!: 25 Great Projects, Activities, Experiments* (Explore Your World). White River Junction, VT: Nomad Press, 2011.

Websites

Due to the changing nature of Internet links, Rosen Publishing has developed an online list of Websites related to the subject of this book. This site is updated regularly. Please use this link to access the list:

http://www.rosenlinks.com/lfo/life

INDEX